PINK FLOYD
THE DARK SIDE OF THE MOON

50° ANNIVERSARIO

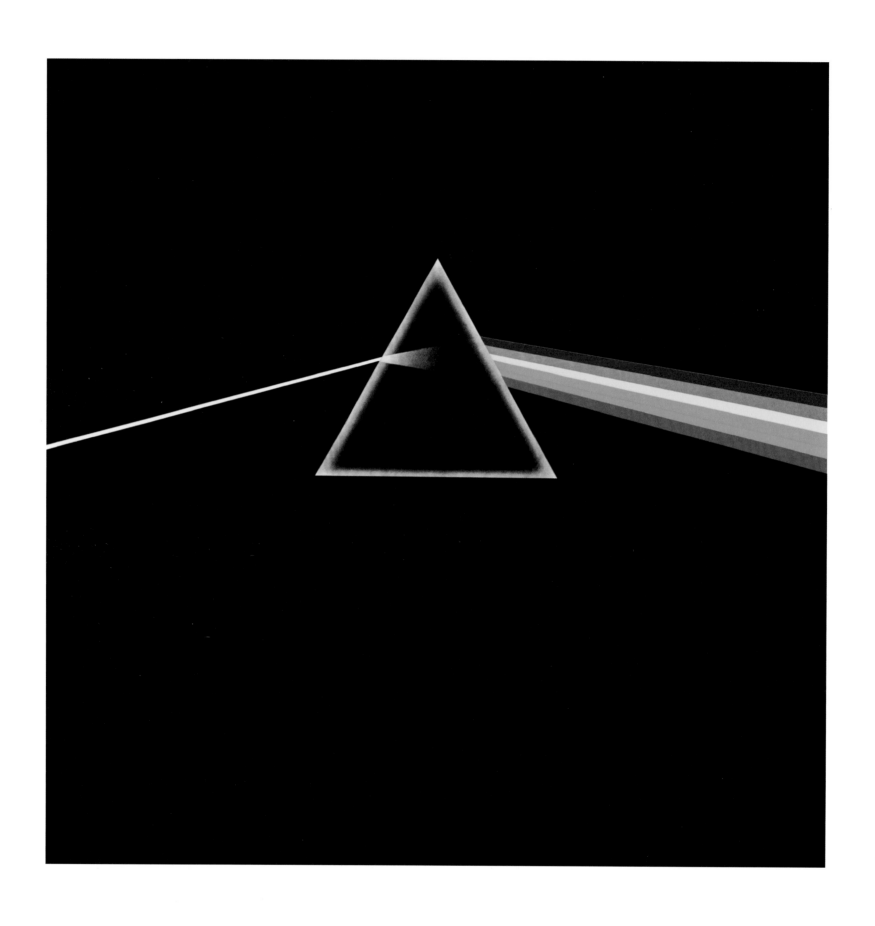

PINK FLOYD
THE DARK SIDE OF THE MOON

50° ANNIVERSARIO

«La luna non ha mica un lato oscuro.
A voler essere precisi, è tutta scura.»

Gerry Driscoll, usciere agli Abbey Road Studios

Rizzoli Lizard

CAUGHT IN THE ACT

PINK FLOYD: world's number one underground band

Floyd's space odyssey

WHILE a host of current bands are injecting glamour and excitement back into rock, the Pink Floyd continue in their own way to do just the opposite. Messrs Waters, Wright, Gilmour and Mason would no sooner wear a satin jacket as finish their set with a rock medley. It's the way it should be, for the Floyd are an institution in this country and elsewhere. They are the world's number one underground band.

And while there are nowadays many who attempt to emulate their space voyage ideas, none are half as good as the Floyd in top gear. They needed no warming up at the Empire Pool,, Wembley, on Saturday. From the word go, they gave the packed stadium a faultless demonstration of what psychedelic music is all about. There wasn't a note, or a sound, out of place during the whole evening.

It's a recital more than a concert, and the Floyd don't so much give us numbers as perform pieces of music, lasting up to an hour each.

For starters on Saturday we had that lengthy work entitled "The Dark Side of the Moon", an eerie title for an equally eerie piece of music that takes the listener through a host of different moods, most of which are accompanied by unusual sounds stretching around his head by way of the group's quadraphonic sound system. I can't understand why more group's don't try this Floydian tactic: the effect is really stunning.

The second half of the recital was composed of three more major pieces, and a couple of encores. The first encore — the riveting "Set The Controls For the Heart of the Sun" — was obviously rehearsed, but the second — a bluesy jam — wasn't. It served a useful purpose to show that the group are not confined to playing science fiction soundtrack music all the time.

The incendiary gimmicks from the stage frequently obliterated the artists. Flasbombs erupted here and there at well-timed places, and Roger Waters' gong actually became a blazing sun during "Controls".

All the time the group were effectively illuminated by their imposing lighting tower at the rear of the stage which served a dual purpose — at frequent intervals it belched out smoke which mingled with the coloured lights and the dry ice surface mist to effectively wisk us all away to Planet Floyd.

Dave Gilmour is an underestimated guitarist. That he knows his instrument back to front is never really in doubt, but playing guitar with the Floyd demands an extra precision, and the ability to strike harsh chords one minute and lighter notes the next. And he has to be the handiest man around when it comes to using an echo chamber, as the extended notes proved.

R.ck Wright, I suspect, contributes considerably more than just keyboards. Someone must dabble around with pre-recorded tapes and Wright seems to be the obvious choice. Both tape and keyboard work is executed with the unassuming precision that typifies the band's approach to their highly individual music.

One final thought: wouldn't it be great if, for once, they dropped the image and played "See Emily Play" — just for an encore.— CHRIS CHARLESWORTH.

L'Odissea nello spazio dei Floyd
PINK FLOYD
la più importante band underground al mondo

Mentre un sacco di band del momento iniettano glamour ed eccitazione nel rock, i Pink Floyd continuano a modo loro a fare l'esatto opposto. Difficilmente vedremo i signori Waters, Wright, Gilmour e Mason indossare una giacca satinata o chiudere un concerto con un medley rock. Ed è giusto che sia così, perché i Floyd sono un'istituzione, in questo Paese come altrove. Sono la più importante band underground al mondo.

E anche se oggi in tanti si sforzano di imitare le loro trovate da viaggio astrale, nessuno vale la metà dei Floyd quando sono in gran tiro. Sabato scorso, alla Empire Pool di Wembley, non hanno avuto bisogno di riscaldarsi. Fin dal primo istante, hanno dimostrato alla folla che riempiva lo stadio che cos'è la musica psichedelica. Durante l'intera serata non si sono sentiti né una nota né un suono fuori posto.

Un recital più che un concerto, perché i Floyd non suonano pezzi, ma vere e proprie composizioni che durano anche un'ora intera.

Come aperitivo, sabato ci hanno servito quella loro lunga creazione chiamata "The Dark Side Of The Moon", un titolo inquietante per un brano altrettanto inquietante, capace di trasportare l'ascoltatore attraverso una lunga serie di stati d'animo, spesso accompagnati da suoni insoliti e avvolgenti, grazie all'impianto quadrifonico della band. Non capisco perché altri gruppi non abbiano ancora adottato questa tattica floydiana: l'effetto è davvero sorprendente.

La seconda parte del recital era composta da altri tre lunghi brani e un paio di bis. Il primo bis (l'avvincente "Set the Controls for the Heart of the Sun") era stato chiaramente provato, a differenza del secondo, una jam dai toni blues, che ha comunque avuto il pregio di dimostrare come la band non sappia suonare solo colonne sonore per film di fantascienza.

Sul palco, gli incendiari effetti di scena rendevano spesso invisibili i musicisti. Lampi di luce esplodevano qua e là, con perfetto tempismo, e durante "Controls" il gong di Roger Waters è diventato un sole fiammeggiante.

Per tutto il concerto il gruppo è stato efficacemente illuminato dall'imponente torre-faro posizionata sul fondo del palco, che aveva una duplice funzione: sputare a intervalli regolari nuvole di fumo che si fondevano con le luci colorate e una leggera foschia da ghiaccio secco, il tutto per spararci dritti sul Pianeta Floyd.

Dave Gilmour è un chitarrista sottovalutato. Nessuno ha mai messo in dubbio che conosca ogni segreto del suo strumento, ma suonare la chitarra nei Floyd richiede una dose extra di precisione e la capacità di eseguire accordi brutali per poi, un attimo dopo, passare a note delicate. E credo che nessuno batta la sua capacità di sfruttare una cassa di risonanza, come dimostrano le sue note prolungate.

Ho inoltre il sospetto che Rick Wright faccia molto di più che suonare le tastiere. C'è di sicuro qualcuno che si diletta con nastri preregistrati e, molto probabilmente, quel qualcuno è proprio Wright. Le tastiere e i nastri sono gestiti con la sottile precisione che ben rappresenta l'approccio della band alla sua musica così originale.

In chiusura, giusto un appunto: non sarebbe bello se, per una volta, la smettessero di fare tante storie e suonassero "See Emily Play", anche solo come bis?

Chris Charlesworth

JOHN SMITH ENTERTAINMENTS
BY ARRANGEMENT WITH STEVE O'ROURKE PRESENT

PINK FLOYD
ON TOUR

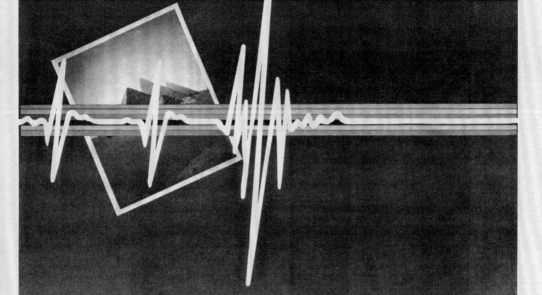

November 4th 1974	Usher Hall, Edinburgh.
5th	
November 8th 1974	Odeon, Newcastle-upon-Tyne.
9th	
November 14th 1974	Empire Pool, Wembley.
15th.	
16th	
November 19th 1974	Trentham Gardens, Stoke-on-Trent
November 22nd 1974	Sophia Gardens, Cardiff.
November 28th 1974	Empire Theatre, Liverpool.
29th	
30th	
December 3rd 1974	Hippodrome, Birmingham.
4th	
5th	
December 9th 1974	Palace Theatre, Manchester.
10th	
December 13th 1974	Hippodrome, Bristol.
14th	

All concerts are at 7.30 in the evening except Wembley—
Wembley evening concerts are at 8.00.

Extra Date: November 17th Empire Pool, Wembley, 6 p.m.

TICKETS ACCEPTED BY MAIL ORDER ONLY UNTIL 7th OCTOBER
LIMITED TO FOUR TICKETS PER PERSON.

SEND STAMPED ADDRESSED ENVELOPE TOGETHER WITH POSTAL
ORDER TO PINK FLOYD CONCERT AT THEATRE BOX OFFICES.

The Dark Side Of The Moon
Date del tour 1972-1975

TOUR DEL REGNO UNITO 1972

20 GENNAIO
The Dome, *Brighton*

21 GENNAIO
Guildhall, *Portsmouth*

22 GENNAIO
Winter Gardens, *Bournemouth*

23 GENNAIO
Guildhall, *Southampton*

27 GENNAIO
City Hall, *Newcastle upon Tyne*

28 GENNAIO
City Hall, *Leeds*

3 FEBBRAIO
Locarno Ballroom, *Coventry*

5 FEBBRAIO
Colston Hall, *Bristol*

10 FEBBRAIO
De Montfort Hall, *Leicester*

12 FEBBRAIO
City Hall, *Sheffield*

13 FEBBRAIO
Empire Theatre, *Liverpool*

17-20 FEBBRAIO
Rainbow Theatre, *Londra*

TOUR DEL GIAPPONE 1972

6-7 MARZO
Tokyo-To Taiikukan, *Shibuya*

8-9 MARZO
Festival Hall, *Osaka*

10 MARZO
Dai-Sho-Gun Furitsu Taiikukan, *Kyoto*

13 MARZO
Nakanoshima Sports Centre, *Sapporo*

REGNO UNITO 1972

29-30 MARZO
Free Trade Hall, *Manchester*

TOUR DEL NORD AMERICA 1972

14 APRILE
Fort Homer W. Hesterly Armory, *Tampa*

15 APRILE
Hollywood Sportatorium,
Pembroke Pines

16 APRILE
Township Auditorium, *Columbia*

18 APRILE
Atlanta Symphony Hall, *Atlanta*

20 APRILE
Syria Mosque Theater, *Pittsburgh*

21 APRILE
Lyric Theater, *Baltimora*

22 APRILE
Civic Theatre, *Akron*

23 APRILE
Music Hall, *Cincinnati*

24 APRILE
Allen Theatre, *Cleveland*

26-27 APRILE
Ford Auditorium, *Detroit*

28 APRILE
Auditorium Theatre, *Chicago*

29 APRILE
Spectrum Theater, *Filadelfia*

1-2 MAGGIO
Carnegie Hall, *New York*

3 MAGGIO
John F. Kennedy Center for the
Performing Arts, *Washington*

4 MAGGIO
Music Hall, *Boston*

TOUR DELL'EUROPA 1972

18 MAGGIO
Deutschlandhalle, *Berlino Ovest,
Germania Ovest*

REGNO UNITO 1972

28-29 GIUGNO
The Dome, *Brighton*

TOUR DEL NORD AMERICA 1972

8 SETTEMBRE
Municipal Auditorium, *Austin*

9 SETTEMBRE
Music Hall, *Houston*

10 SETTEMBRE
McFarlin Auditorium, *Dallas*

11 SETTEMBRE
Memorial Hall, *Kansas City*

12 SETTEMBRE
Civic Center Music Hall, *Oklahoma City*

13 SETTEMBRE
Henry Levitt Arena, *Wichita*

15 SETTEMBRE
Community Center Arena, *Tucson*

16 SETTEMBRE
Golden Hall, *San Diego*

17 SETTEMBRE
Big Surf, *Tempe*

19 SETTEMBRE
University of Denver Arena, *Denver*

22 SETTEMBRE
Hollywood Bowl, *Los Angeles*

23-24 SETTEMBRE
Winterland Auditorium, *San Francisco*

27 SETTEMBRE
Garden Auditorium, *Vancouver*

28 SETTEMBRE
Memorial Coliseum, *Portland*

29 SETTEMBRE
Hec Edmundson Pavilion, *Seattle*

30 SETTEMBRE
Garden Auditorium, *Vancouver*

REGNO UNITO 1972

21 OTTOBRE
Wembley Empire Pool, *Londra*

TOUR DELL'EUROPA 1972

10-11 NOVEMBRE
Kb Hallen, *Copenaghen, Danimarca*

12 NOVEMBRE
Ernst-Merck-Halle, *Amburgo,
Germania Ovest*

14 NOVEMBRE
Philipshalle, *Düsseldorf, Germania Ovest*

15 NOVEMBRE
Sporthalle, *Böblingen, Germania Ovest*

16-17 NOVEMBRE
Festhalle, *Francoforte, Germania Ovest*

28 NOVEMBRE
Palais des Sports, *Tolosa, Francia*

29 NOVEMBRE
Parc des Expositions, *Poitiers, Francia*

1-2 DICEMBRE
Centre Sportif de L'île de Vannes,
Parigi, Francia

3 DICEMBRE
Parc des Expositions, *Caen, Francia*

5 DICEMBRE
Vorst Nationaal, *Bruxelles, Belgio*

7 DICEMBRE
Palais des Sports, *Lille, Francia*

8 DICEMBRE
Parc des Expositions, *Nancy, Francia*

9 DICEMBRE
Hallenstadion, *Zurigo, Svizzera*

10 DICEMBRE
Palais des Sports, *Lione, Francia*

TOUR DEL NORD AMERICA 1973

4 MARZO
Dane County Memorial Coliseum,
Madison

5 MARZO
Cobo Arena, *Detroit*

6 MARZO
Kiel Opera House, *Saint Louis*

7 MARZO
International Amphitheatre, *Chicago*

8 MARZO
Armory Fieldhouse, *Cincinnati*

10 MARZO
Memorial Gymnasium, *Kent*

11 MARZO
Maple Leaf Gardens, *Toronto*

12 MARZO
Forum de Montréal, *Montréal*

14 MARZO
Music Hall, *Boston*

15 MARZO
Spectrum Theater, *Filadelfia*

17 MARZO
Radio City Music Hall, *New York*

18 MARZO
Palace Theater, *Waterbury*

19 MARZO
Providence Civic Center, *Providence*

22 MARZO
Hampton Coliseum, *Hampton*

23 MARZO
Charlotte Park Center, *Charlotte*

24 MARZO
Municipal Auditorium, *Atlanta*

REGNO UNITO 1973

18-19 MAGGIO
Earls Court, *Londra*

TOUR DEL NORD AMERICA 1973

17 GIUGNO
Saratoga Performing Arts Center,
Saratoga

18 GIUGNO
Roosevelt Stadium, *Jersey City*

19 GIUGNO
Civic Center Arena, *Pittsburgh*

20-21 GIUGNO
Merriweather Post Pavilion, *Columbia*

22 GIUGNO
Buffalo Memorial Auditorium, *Buffalo*

23 GIUGNO
Olympia Stadium, *Detroit*

24 GIUGNO
Blossom Music Center, *Cuyahoga*

25 GIUGNO
Convention Center, *Louisville*

27 GIUGNO
Jacksonville Coliseum, *Jacksonville*

28 GIUGNO
Hollywood Sportatorium,
Pembroke Pines

29 GIUGNO
Tampa Stadium, *Tampa*

EUROPA 1973

12 OTTOBRE
Münchener Olympiahalle,
Monaco, Germania Ovest

13 OTTOBRE
Stadthalle, *Vienna, Austria*

REGNO UNITO 1973

4 NOVEMBRE, ore 17 e ore 21
Rainbow Theatre, *Londra*

TOUR DELLA FRANCIA 1974

18 GIUGNO
Palais des Expositions, *Tolosa*

19 GIUGNO
Parc des Expositions, *Poitiers*

21 GIUGNO
Parc des Expositions, *Digione*

22 GIUGNO
Théâtre de Plein Air, Parc des
Expositions, *Colmar*

24-26 GIUGNO
Palais des Sports, *Parigi*

TOUR INVERNALE DELLA
GRAN BRETAGNA 1974

4-5 NOVEMBRE
Usher Hall, *Edimburgo*

8-9 NOVEMBRE
Odeon, *Newcastle upon Tyne*

14-17 NOVEMBRE
Wembley Empire Pool, *Londra*

19 NOVEMBRE
Trentham Gardens, *Stoke-on-Trent*

22 NOVEMBRE
Sophia Gardens Pavilion, *Cardiff*

28-30 NOVEMBRE
Empire Theatre, *Liverpool*

3-5 DICEMBRE
The Hippodrome, *Birmingham*

9-10 DICEMBRE
The Palace Theatre, *Manchester*

13-14 DICEMBRE
The Hippodrome, *Bristol*

TOUR DEL NORD AMERICA 1975

8 APRILE
Pacific National Exhibition Coliseum,
Vancouver

10 APRILE
Seattle Center Coliseum, *Seattle*

12-13 APRILE
Cow Palace, *San Francisco*

17 APRILE
Denver Coliseum, *Denver*

19 APRILE
Tucson Community Center, *Tucson*

20 APRILE
University Activity Center, *Tempe*

21 APRILE
Sports Arena, *San Diego*

22-27 APRILE
Los Angeles Memorial Sports Arena,
Los Angeles

7 GIUGNO
Atlanta Stadium, *Atlanta*

10 GIUGNO
Capital Center, *Landover*

12-13 GIUGNO
Spectrum Theater, *Filadelfia*

14 GIUGNO
Roosevelt Stadium, *Jersey City*

16-17 GIUGNO
Nassau Veterans Memorial Coliseum,
Uniondale

18 GIUGNO
Boston Garden, *Boston*

20 GIUGNO
Three Rivers Stadium, *Pittsburgh*

22 GIUGNO
County Stadium, *Milwaukee*

23-24 GIUGNO
Olympia Stadium, *Detroit*

26 GIUGNO
Autostade, *Montréal*

28 GIUGNO
Ivor Wynne Stadium, *Hamilton*

REGNO UNITO 1975

5 LUGLIO
Knebworth Park, *Stevenage*

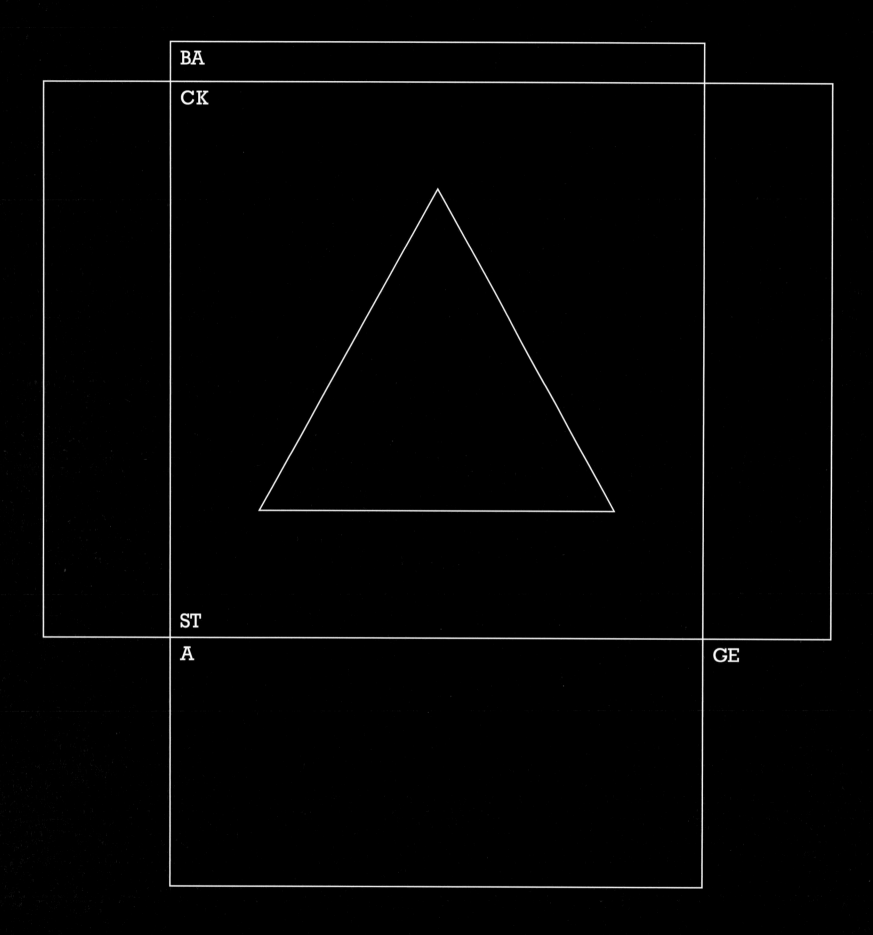

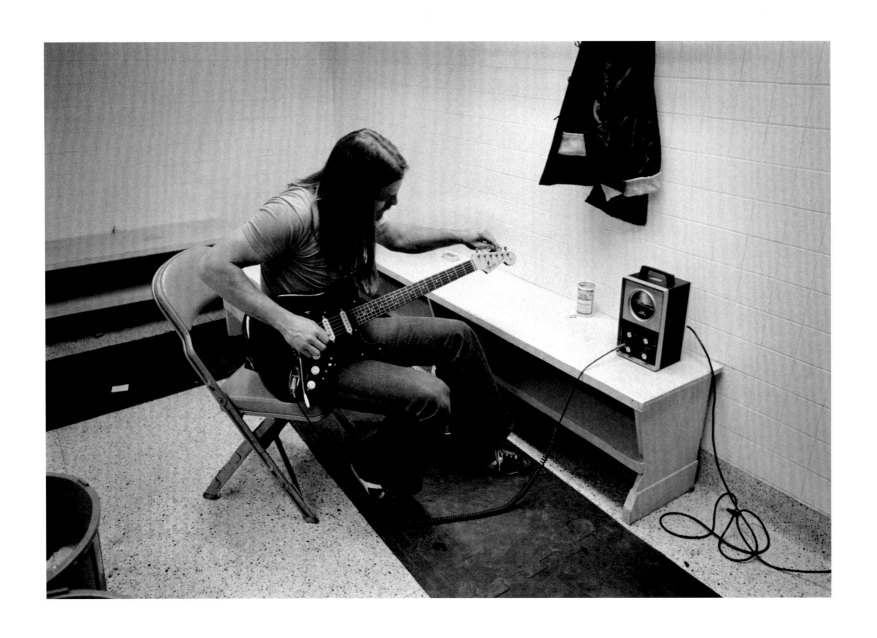

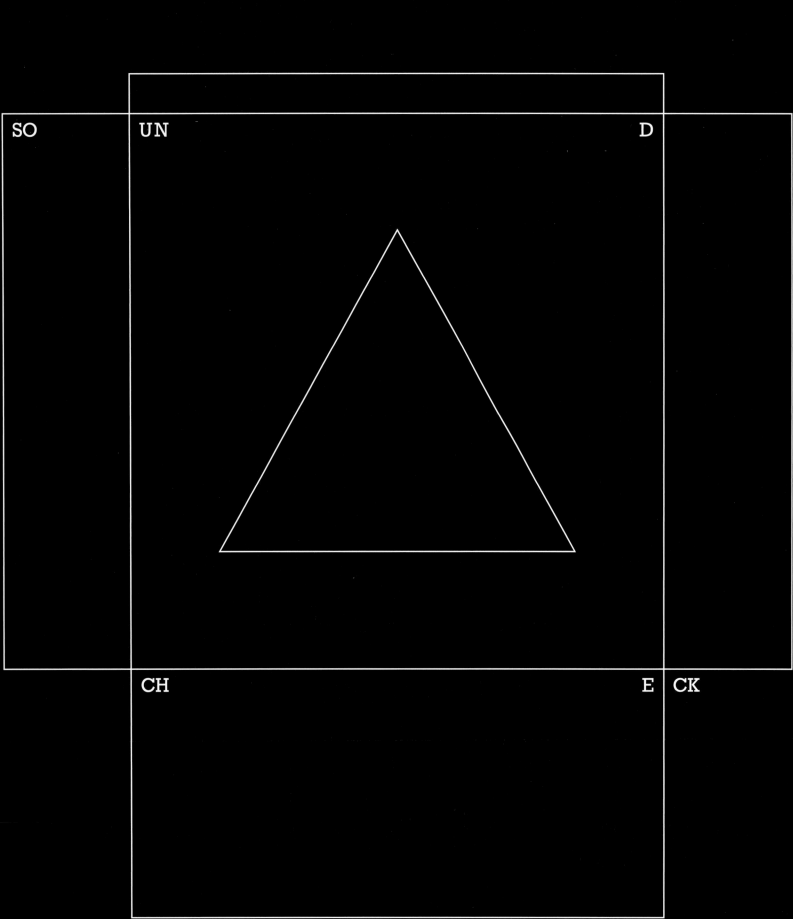

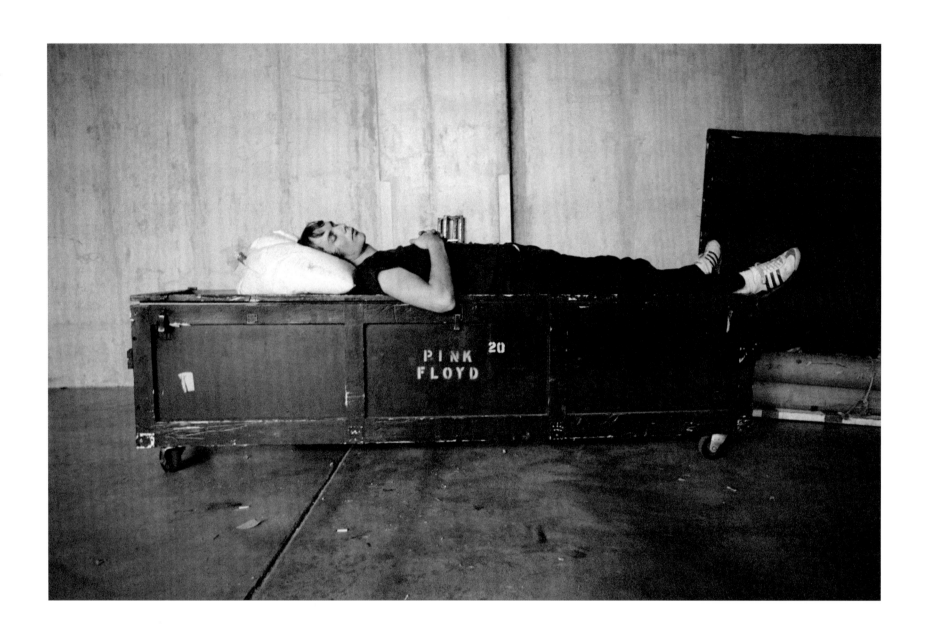

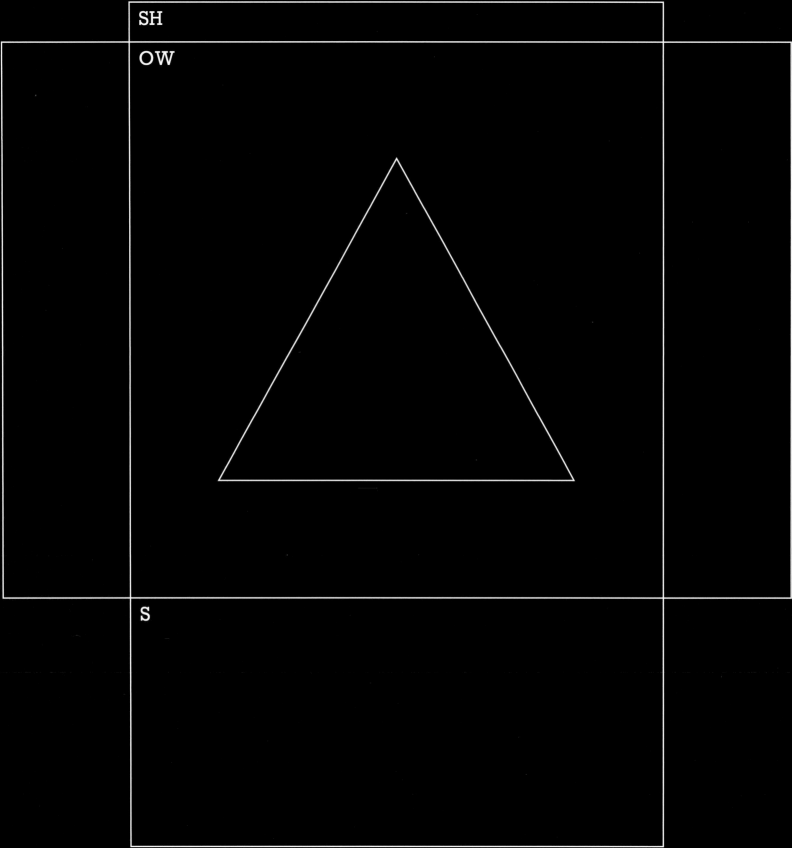

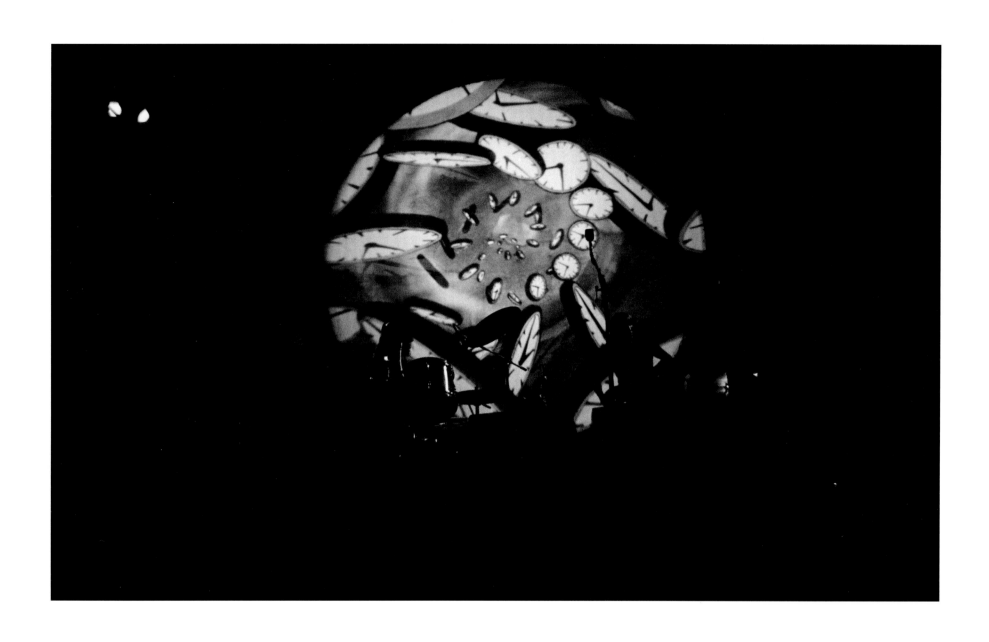

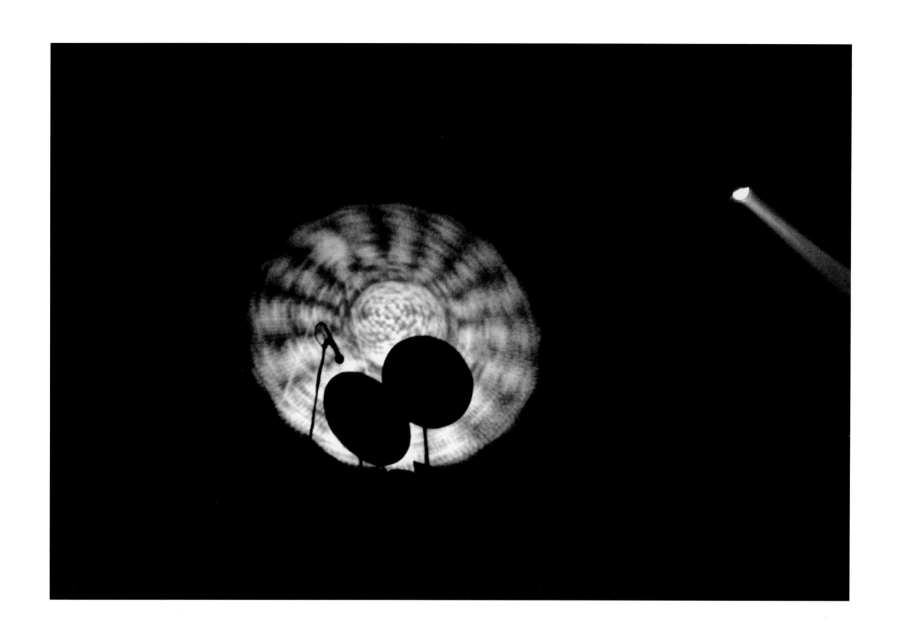

AF

TE
R

SH OW

ART
WO

RK
S

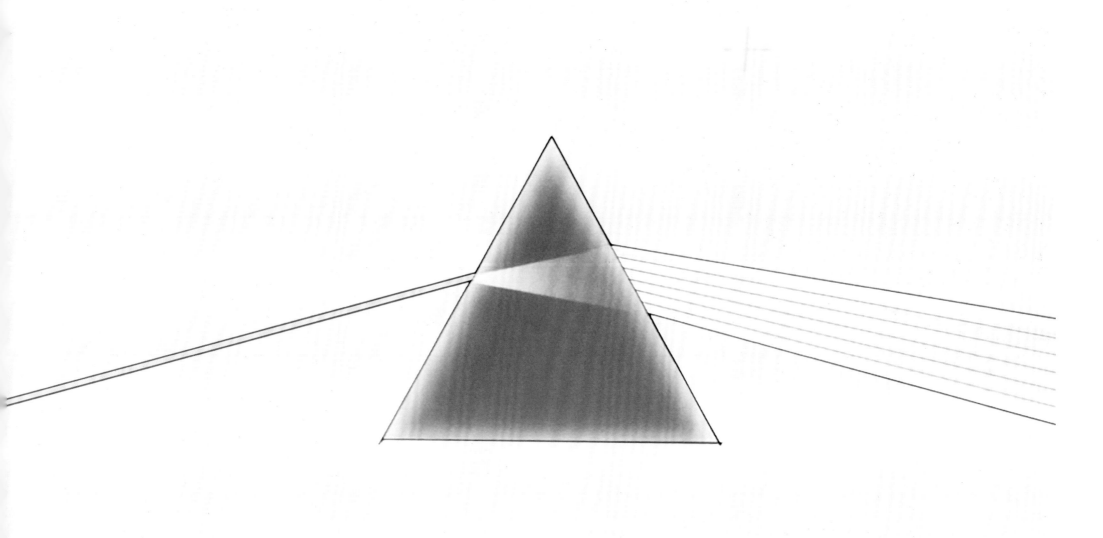

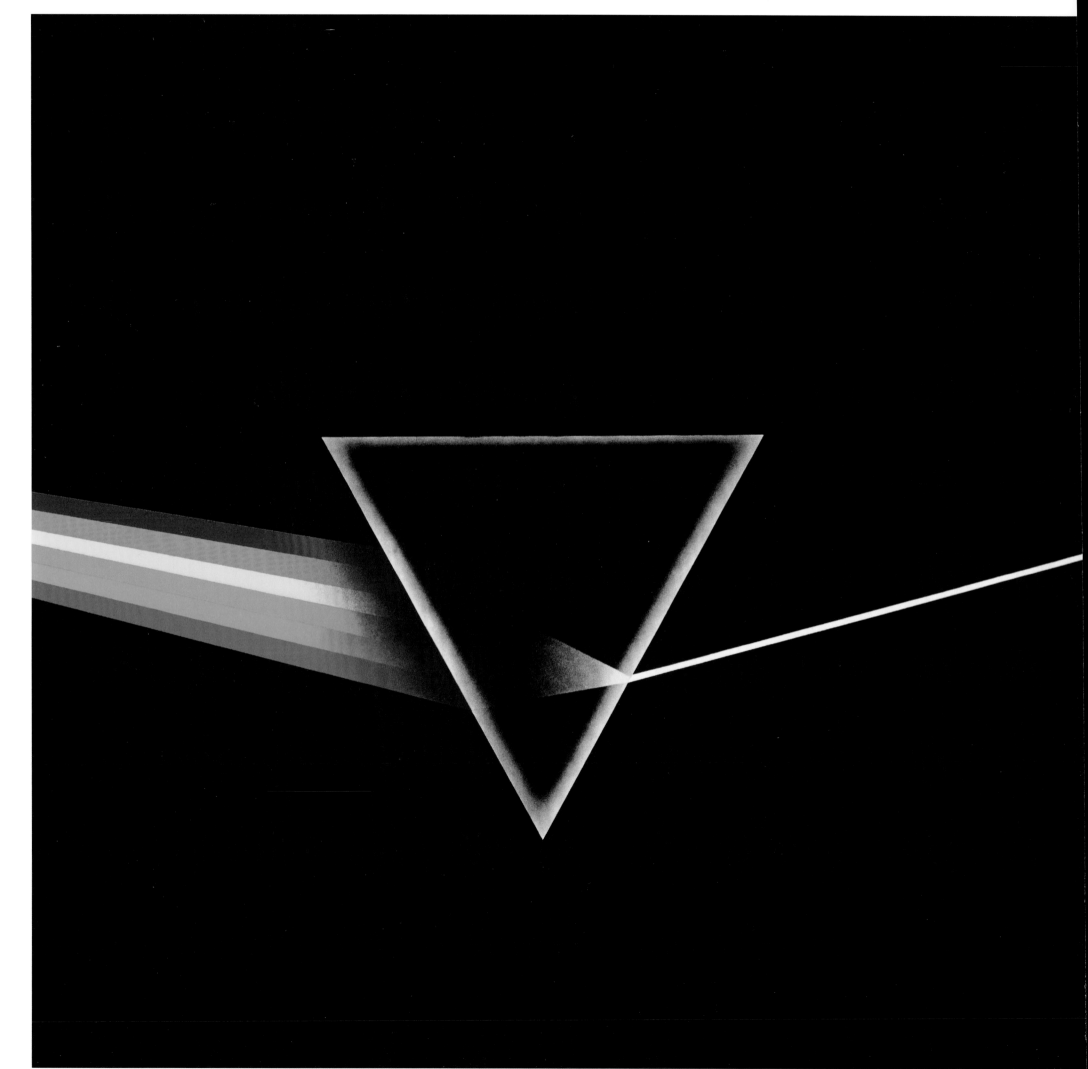

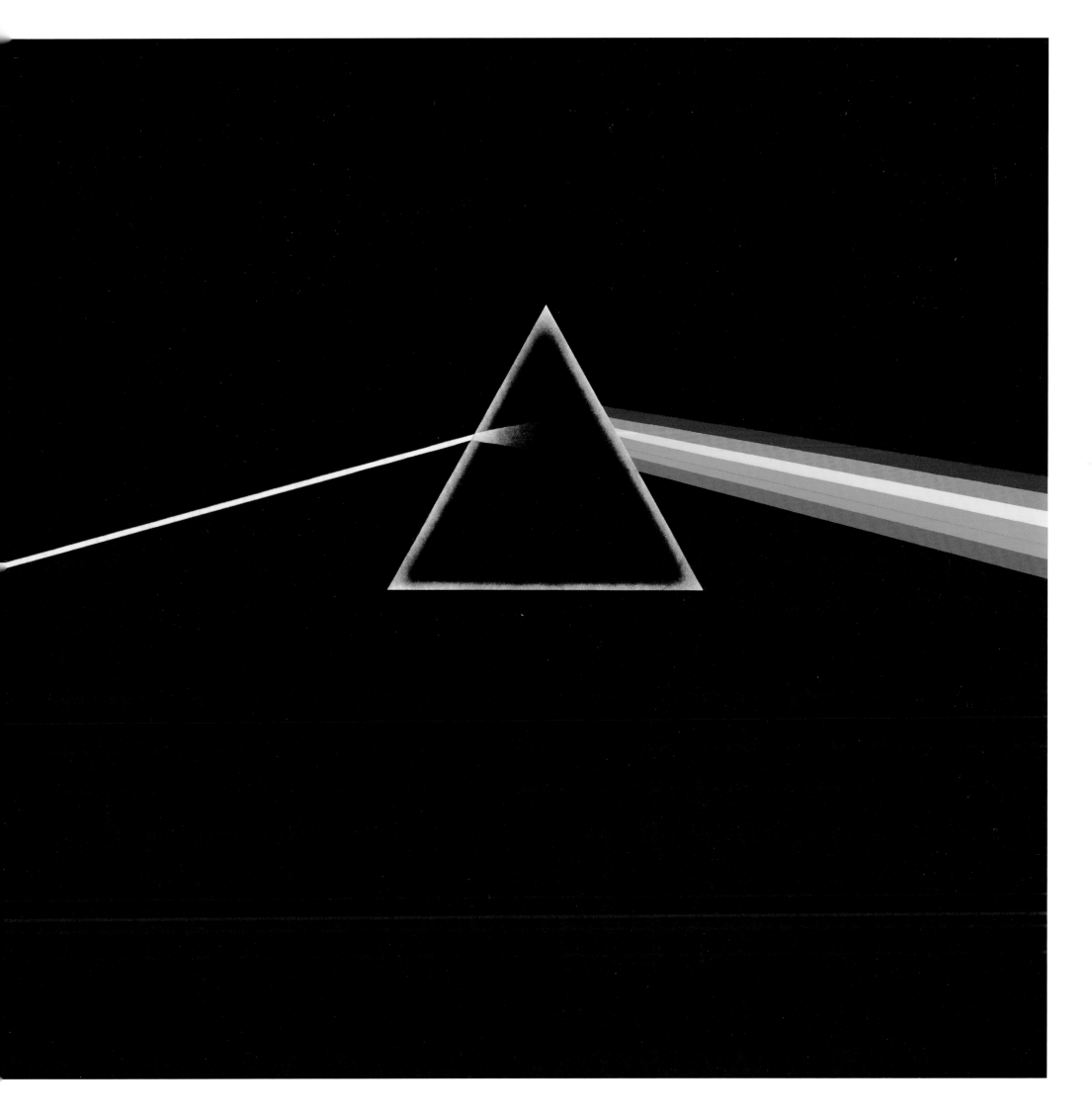

PINK FLOYD

INSIDE COVER

ALL BACKGROUND UP TO KEYLINES TO PRINT SOLID BLACK. BLACK + 80% CYAN

DROP IN SIX COLOUR TINTS AS SHOWN ON THIS OVERLAY.

* NO KEYLINES TO APPEAR

USE THE SAME SIX COLOUR TINTS FOR FRONT & BACK COVER.

SIDE ONE
1 SPEAK TO ME (Mason)
2 BREATHE (Waters, Gilmour, Wright)
3 ON THE RUN (Gilmour, Waters)
4 TIME (Mason, Waters, Wright, Gilmour)
5 THE GREAT GIG IN THE SKY (Wright)

SIDE TWO
1 MONEY (Waters)
2 US AND THEM (Waters, Wright)
3 ANY COLOUR YOU LIKE (Gilmour, Mason, Wright)
4 BRAIN DAMAGE (Waters)
5 ECLIPSE (waters)

DAVID GILMOUR Vocals, Guitars, VCS3
NICK MASON Percussion, Tape Effects
RICHARD WRIGHT Keyboards, Vocals, VCS3
ROGER WATERS Bass Guitar, Vocals, VCS3, Tape Effects

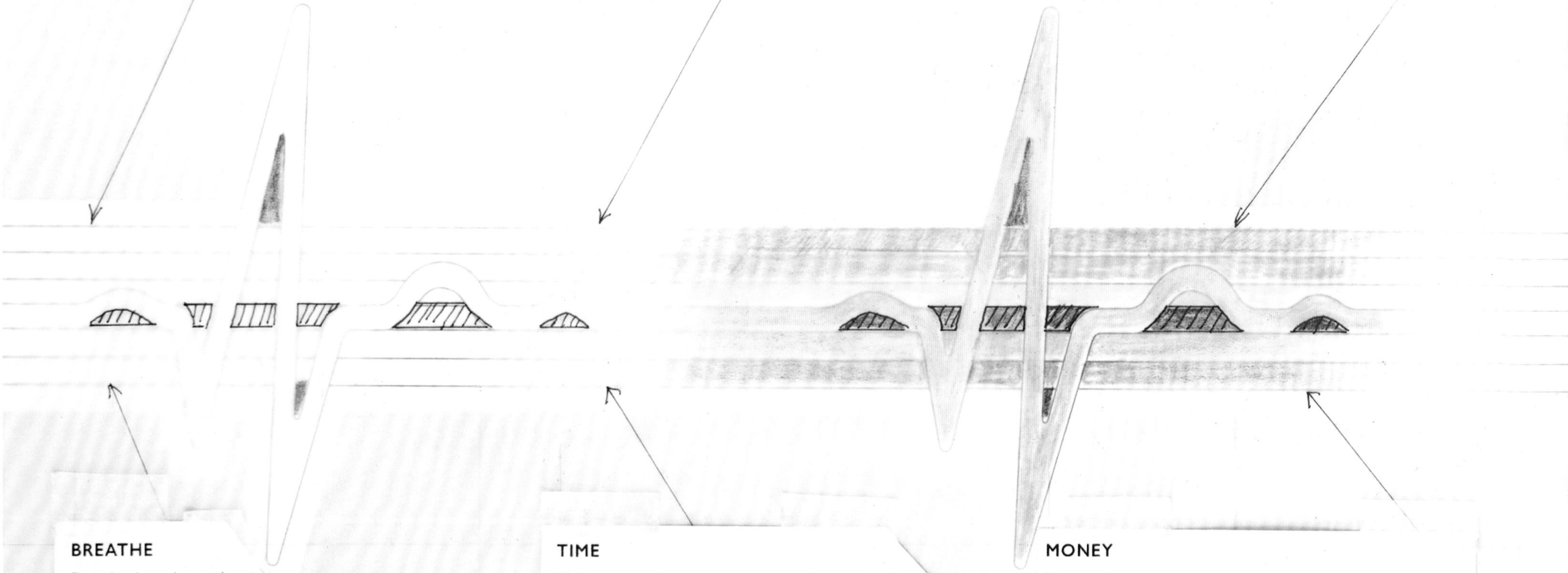

BREATHE

Breathe, breathe in the air
Don't be afraid to care
Leave, don't leave me
Walk around and choose your own ground
Long you live and high you fly
Smiles you'll give and tears you'll cry
All you touch and all you see
Is all your life will ever be

Run, rabbit, run
Dig that hole, forget the sun
And when at last the work is done
Don't sit down it's time to dig another one
For long you'll live, and high you'll fly
But only if you ride the tide
And balanced on the biggest wave
You race towards an early grave.

TIME

Ticking away the moments that make up a dull day
Fritter and waste the hours in an offhand way
Kicking around on a piece of ground in your hometown
Waiting for someone or something to show you the way

Tired of lying in the sunshine, staying home to watch the rain
You are young and life is long, and there is time to kill today
And then one day you find ten years have got behind you
No one told you when to run, you missed the starting gun

And you run, and you run to catch up with the sun but it's sinking
Racing around to come up behind you again
The sun is the same in a relative way but you're older
Shorter of breath and one day closer to death

Every year is getting shorter, never seem to find the time
Plans that either come to naught or half a page of scribbled lines
Hanging on in quiet desperation is the English way
The time is gone, the song is over, thought I'd something more to say

Breathe Reprise

Home, home again
I like to be here when I can
And when I come home cold and tired
It's good to warm my bones beside the fire
Far away across the field
The tolling of the iron bell
Calls the faithful to their knees
To hear the softly spoken magic spells.

MONEY

Money, Get away
Get a good job with more pay and you're O.K.
Money, it's a gas
Grab that cash with both hands and make a stash
New car, caviar, four star daydream
Think I'll buy me a football team

Money, get back
I'm alright Jack, keep your hands off of my stack
Money, it's a hit
Don't give me that do goody good bullshit
I'm in the hi-fidelity first class traveling set
And I think I need a Lear jet

Money, it's a crime
Share it fairly, but don't take a slice of my pie
Money, so they say
Is the root of all evil today
But if you ask for a rise it's no surprise that they're
giving none away

Produced by PINK FLOYD
Recorded at Abbey Road Studios, London
between June 1972 and January 1973

Engineer Alan Parsons
Assistant Peter James
Mixing Supervised by Chris Thomas

Saxophone on 'Us and Them' and 'Money' by Dick Parry

Vocals on 'The Great Gig in the Sky' by Clare Torry
Backing Vocals Doris Troy,
Leslie Duncan, Liza Strike, Barry St John

Sleeve Design by Hipgnosis
Sleeve Art by George Hardie N.T.A.
Photography buy Hipgnosis
Stickers Art by George Hardie N.T.A.

All lyrics by ROGER WATERS

℗ 1973 Also available on cassette and cartridge

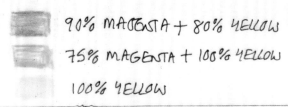

90% MAGENTA + 80% YELLOW

75% MAGENTA + 100% YELLOW

100% YELLOW

70% CYAN + 20% MAGENTA + 100% YELLOW

90% CYAN + 25% MAGENTA + 15% YELLOW

70% CYAN + 80% MAGENTA

REVERSE ALL CREDITS,
TRACK LIST & LYRICS TO
WHITE OUT OF SOLID BLACK

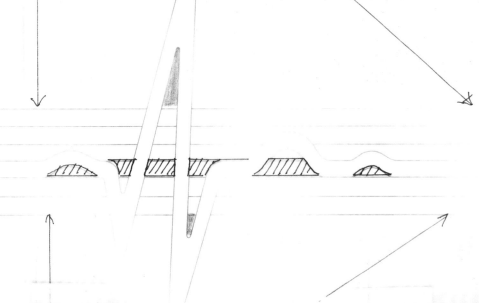

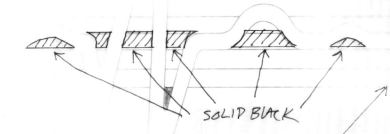

SOLID BLACK

US AND THEM

Us, and them
And after all we're only ordinary men
Me, and you
God only knows
It's not what we would choose to do
Forward he cried from the rear
And the front rank died
And the General sat, and the lines on the map
moved from side to side
Black and blue
And who knows which is which and who is who
Up and Down
And in the end it's only round and round and round
Haven't you heard it's a battle of words
the poster bearer cried
Listen son, said the man with the gun
There's room for you inside

Down and Out
It can't be helped but there's a lot of it about
With, without
And who'll deny it's what the fighting's all about
Out of the way, it's a busy day
I've got things on my mind
For the want of the price of tea and a slice
The old man died

BRAIN DAMAGE

The lunatic is on the grass
The lunatic is on the grass
Remembering games and daisy chains and laughs
Got to keep the loonies on the path

The lunatic is in the hall
The lunatics are in my hall
The paper holds their folded faces to the floor
And every day the paper boy brings more

And if the dam breaks open many years too soon
And if there is no room upon the hill
And if your head explodes with dark forebodings too
I'll see you on the dark side of the moon

The lunatic is in my head
The lunatic is in my head
You raise the blade, you make the change
You re-arrange me 'til I'm sane

You lock the door
And throw away the key
There's someone in my head but it's not me.

And if the cloud bursts, thunder in your ear
You shout and no one seems to hear
And if the band you're in starts playing different tunes
I'll see you on the dark side of the moon

ECLIPSE

All that you touch
And all that you see
All that you taste
All you feel
And all that you love
And all that you hate
All you distrust
All you save
All that you give
All that you deal
All that you buy
beg, borrow or steal
All you create
All you destroy
All that you do
All that you say
All that you eat
everyone you meet
All that you slight
everyone you fight
All that is now
All that is gone
All that's to come
and everything under the sun is in tune
but the sun is eclipsed by the moon.

SIDE ONE
1 SPEAK TO ME (Mason)
2 BREATHE (Waters, Gilmour, Wright)
3 ON THE RUN (Gilmour, Waters)
4 TIME (Mason, Waters, Wright, Gilmour)
5 THE GREAT GIG IN THE SKY (Wright)

SIDE TWO
1 MONEY (Waters)
2 US AND THEM (Waters, Wright)
3 ANY COLOUR YOU LIKE (Gilmour, Mason, Wright)
4 BRAIN DAMAGE (Waters)
5 ECLIPSE (Waters)

DAVID GILMOUR Vocals, Guitars, VCS3
NICK MASON Percussion, Tape Effects
RICHARD WRIGHT Keyboards, Vocals, VCS3
ROGER WATERS Bass Guitar, Vocals, VCS3, Tape Effects

BREATHE

Breathe, breathe in the air
Don't be afraid to care
Leave but don't leave me
Look around and choose your own ground
For long you live and high you fly
And smiles you'll give and tears you'll cry
And all you touch and all you see
Is all your life will ever be

Run rabbit run
Dig that hole, forget the sun,
And when at last the work is done
Don't sit down it's time to start another one
For long you live and high you fly
But only if you ride the tide
And balanced on the biggest wave
You race toward an early grave.

TIME

Ticking away the moments that make up a dull day
You fritter and waste the hours in an off hand way
Kicking around on a piece of ground in your home town
Waiting for someone or something to show you the way

Tired of lying in the sunshine staying home to watch the rain
You are young and life is long and there is time to kill today
And then one day you find ten years have got behind you
No one told you when to run, you missed the starting gun

And you run and you run to catch up with the sun, but it's sinking
And racing around to come up behind you again
The sun is the same in the relative way, but you're older
Shorter of breath and one day closer to death

Every year is getting shorter, never seem to find the time
Plans that either come to naught or half a page of scribbled lines
Hanging on in quiet desperation is the English way
The time is gone the song is over, thought I'd something more to say

Breathe Reprise

Home, home again
I like to be here when I can
When I come home cold and tired
It's good to warm my bones beside the fire
Far away across the field
The tolling of the iron bell
Calls the faithful to their knees
To hear the softly spoken magic spells.

MONEY

Money, get away
Get a good job with more pay and your O.K.
Money it's a gas
Grab that cash with both hands and make a stash
New car, caviar, four star daydream,
Think I'll buy me a football team

Money get back
I'm all right Jack keep your hands of my stack.
Money it's a hit
Don't give me that do goody good bullshit
I'm in the hi-fidelity first class travelling set
And I think I need a Lear jet

Money it's a crime
Share it fairly but don't take a slice of my pie
Money so they say
Is the root of all evil today
But if you ask for a rise it's no surprise that they're
giving none away

E.M.I RECORDS (The Gramophone Company Ltd)
HAYES MIDDLESEX ENGLAND

File under POPULAR : Pop Groups

Made and printed in the EU

7303   TPS

SHVL 804

Produced by PINK FLOYD
Recorded at Abbey Road Studios, London
between June 1972 and January 1973

Engineer Alan Parsons
Assistant Peter James
Mixing Supervised by Chris Thomas

Saxophone on 'Us and Them' and 'Money' Dick Parry

Vocals on 'The Great Gig in the Sky' by Clare Torry
Backing Vocals Doris Troy,
Leslie Duncan, Liza Strike, Barry St John

Sleeve Design by Hipgnosis
Sleeve Art by George Hardie N.T.A.
Photography by Hipgnosis
Stickers Art by George Hardie N.T.A.

All lyrics by ROGER WATERS.

US AND THEM

Us, and them
And after all we're only ordinary men
Me, and you
God only knows it's not what we would choose to do
Forward he cried from the rear
and the front rank died
And the General sat, and the lines on the map
moved from side to side
Black and blue
And who knows which is which and who is who
Up and Down
And in the end it's only round and round and round
Haven't you heard it's a battle of words
the poster bearer cried
Listen son, said the man with the gun
There's room for you inside

Down and Out
It can't be helped but there's a lot of it about
With, without
And who'll deny it's what the fighting's all about
Out of the way, it's a busy day
I've got things on my mind
For want of the price of tea and a slice
The old man died

BRAIN DAMAGE

The lunatic is on the grass
The lunatic is on the grass
Remembering games and daisy chains and laughs
Got to keep the loonies on the path

The lunatic is in the hall
The lunatics are in my hall
The paper holds their folded faces to the floor
And every day the paper boy brings more

And if the dam breaks open many years too soon
And if there is no room upon the hill
And if your head explodes with dark forbodings too
I'll see you on the dark side of the moon

The lunatic is in my head
The lunatic is in my head
You raise the blade, you make the change
You re-arrange me 'till I'm sane

You lock the door
And throw away the key
There's someone in my head but it's not me.

And if the cloud bursts, thunder in your ear
You shout and no one seems to hear
And if the band you're in starts playing different tunes
I'll see you on the dark side of the moon.

ECLIPSE

All that you touch
All that you see
All that you taste
All you feel
All that you love
All that you hate
All you distrust
All you save
All that you give
All that you deal
All that you buy
beg, borrow or steal
All you create
All you destroy
All that you do
All that you say
All that you eat
everyone you meet
All that you slight
everyone you fight
All that is now
All that is gone
All that's to come
and everything under the sun is in tune
but the sun is eclipsed by the moon.

Didascalie e
Crediti fotografici

02   COPERTINA DELL'ALBUM 1973
Hipgnosis | George Hardie

04   PINK FLOYD 1971, *Richard Wright,
David Gilmour, Nick Mason* e *Roger Waters*
a Belsize Park, Londra, Regno Unito.
Pink Floyd Music Ltd

05   PINK FLOYD 1971, *Richard Wright,
Roger Waters, Nick Mason* e *David Gilmour*
a Belsize Park, Londra, Regno Unito.
Pink Floyd Music Ltd

06   RITAGLIO DI GIORNALE, 1972,
la recensione di Chris Charlesworth del
concerto alla Wembley Empire Pool, Londra,
Regno Unito, apparsa su «Melody Maker»
il 28 ottobre 1972.
Pink Floyd Archive

07   OTTOBRE 1974, Una pagina del «New
Musical Express» con le date del tour in
Gran Bretagna di novembre e dicembre 1974.
Pink Floyd Archive

BACKSTAGE

11   GIUGNO 1972, *Richard Wright, Nick
Mason, Roger Waters* e *David Gilmour* nel
backstage del Dome, Brighton, Regno Unito.
Jill Furmanovsky Archive

12   GIUGNO 1972, *Richard Wright, Nick
Mason* e il sound designer *Bill Kelsey* nel
backstage del Dome, Brighton, Regno Unito.
Jill Furmanovsky Archive

13   GIUGNO 1972, *Roger Waters* e *David
Gilmour* nel backstage del Dome, Brighton,
Regno Unito.
Jill Furmanovsky Archive

14   NOVEMBRE 1974, *Nick Mason*, con una
maglietta «Lucky Shifts», nel backstage della
Usher Hall, Edimburgo, Regno Unito.
Jill Furmanovsky Archive

15   APRILE 1975, *Roger Waters* nel
backstage della Los Angeles Memorial Sports
Arena, Stati Uniti.
*Storm Thorgerson and Aubrey "Po" Powell,
Hipgnosis, Pink Floyd Music Ltd*

16   NOVEMBRE 1974, *David Gilmour*
nel backstage della Usher Hall, Edimburgo,
Regno Unito.
Jill Furmanovsky Archive

17   DICEMBRE 1974, *Richard Wright*
fotografato dal designer dello studio
Hipgnosis *Aubrey "Po" Powell* nel backstage
dell'Hippodrome, Birmingham, Regno Unito.
*Storm Thorgerson and Aubrey "Po" Powell,
Hipgnosis, Pink Floyd Music Ltd*

18   NOVEMBRE 1974, il sassofonista
Dick Parry e il fotografo *Peter Christopherson*
nel backstage dell'Empire Theatre, Liverpool,
Regno Unito.
*Storm Thorgerson and Aubrey "Po" Powell,
Hipgnosis, Pink Floyd Music Ltd*

19   NOVEMBRE 1974, *Nick Mason* e la
fotografa del rock *Jill Furmanovsky* guardano

delle diapositive nel backstage dell'Empire
Theatre, Liverpool, Regno Unito.
*Storm Thorgerson and Aubrey "Po" Powell,
Hipgnosis, Pink Floyd Music Ltd*

20   NOVEMBRE 1974, *Nick Mason* e la
corista *Carlena Williams* nel backstage
dell'Empire Theatre, Liverpool, Regno Unito.
*Storm Thorgerson and Aubrey "Po" Powell,
Hipgnosis, Pink Floyd Music Ltd*

21   APRILE 1975, *Roger Waters* e la corista
Venetta Fields nel backstage della Los Angeles
Memorial Sports Arena, Stati Uniti.
*Storm Thorgerson and Aubrey "Po" Powell,
Hipgnosis, Pink Floyd Music Ltd*

22   DICEMBRE 1974, le coriste *Carlena
Williams* e *Venetta Fields* nel backstage del
Palace Theatre, Manchester, Regno Unito.
*Storm Thorgerson and Aubrey "Po" Powell,
Hipgnosis, Pink Floyd Music Ltd*

23   APRILE 1975, *Nick Mason* e due giovani
familiari dello staff del tour nel backstage
della Los Angeles Memorial Sports Arena,
Stati Uniti.
*Storm Thorgerson and Aubrey "Po" Powell,
Hipgnosis, Pink Floyd Music Ltd*

24   APRILE 1975, *Storm Thorgerson,*
designer dello studio Hipgnosis, nel
backstage della Los Angeles Memorial Sports
Arena, Stati Uniti.
*Storm Thorgerson and Aubrey "Po" Powell,
Hipgnosis, Pink Floyd Music Ltd*

25   DICEMBRE 1974, *Roger Waters,
David Gilmour* e il designer dello studio
Hipgnosis *Aubrey "Po" Powell* nel
backstage dell'Hippodrome, Birmingham,
Regno Unito.
Jill Furmanovsky Archive

26   DICEMBRE 1974, *Nick Mason, Roger
Waters, Richard Wright, David Gilmour*
e l'amico della band *Nick Sedgwick* nel
backstage dell'Hippodrome, Birmingham,
Regno Unito.
*Storm Thorgerson and Aubrey "Po" Powell,
Hipgnosis, Pink Floyd Music Ltd*

27   NOVEMBRE 1974, *David Gilmour,
Roger Waters, Richard Wright, Nick Mason*
e la corista *Carlena Williams* leggono
il «Melody Maker» (*Bad Company Lifts
Off!*) nel backstage dell'Empire Theatre,
Liverpool, Regno Unito.
*Storm Thorgerson and Aubrey "Po" Powell,
Hipgnosis, Pink Floyd Music Ltd*

28   NOVEMBRE 1974, *Richard Wright,
David Gilmour* e *Roger Waters* giocano a
backgammon con l'amico della band *Nick
Sedgwick* nel backstage della Usher Hall,
Edimburgo, Regno Unito.
*Storm Thorgerson and Aubrey "Po" Powell,
Hipgnosis, Pink Floyd Music Ltd*

29   APRILE 1975, *Roger Waters* e *David
Gilmour* nel backstage della Los Angeles
Memorial Sports Arena, Stati Uniti.
*Storm Thorgerson and Aubrey "Po" Powell,
Hipgnosis, Pink Floyd Music Ltd*

30   APRILE 1975, *David Gilmour, Richard
Wright, Roger Waters* e l'amico della band
Nick Sedgwick nel backstage del Pacific
Coliseum, Vancouver, Canada.
*Storm Thorgerson and Aubrey "Po" Powell,
Hipgnosis, Pink Floyd Music Ltd*

31   NOVEMBRE 1974, *Roger Waters* e
Richard Wright nel backstage dell'Empire
Theatre, Liverpool, Regno Unito.
*Storm Thorgerson and Aubrey "Po" Powell,
Hipgnosis, Pink Floyd Music Ltd*

32   NOVEMBRE 1974, *Richard Wright*
e *Juliette Gale*, sua moglie all'epoca, nel
backstage dell'Empire Theatre, Liverpool,
Regno Unito.
*Storm Thorgerson and Aubrey "Po" Powell,
Hipgnosis, Pink Floyd Music Ltd*

33   NOVEMBRE 1974, *Nick Mason* e
David Gilmour nel backstage dell'Empire
Theatre, Liverpool, Regno Unito.
*Storm Thorgerson and Aubrey "Po" Powell,
Hipgnosis, Pink Floyd Music Ltd*

34   NOVEMBRE 1974, *David Gilmour*
e *Richard Wright* nel backstage dell'Empire
Theatre, Liverpool, Regno Unito.
*Storm Thorgerson and Aubrey "Po" Powell,
Hipgnosis, Pink Floyd Music Ltd*

35   NOVEMBRE 1974, *Nick Mason* imita
il comico americano *Jimmy Durante* vicino
all'amico della band *Nick Sedgwick*, nel
backstage della Usher Hall, Edimburgo,
Regno Unito.
*Storm Thorgerson and Aubrey "Po" Powell,
Hipgnosis, Pink Floyd Music Ltd*

36   APRILE 1975, *David Gilmour* accorda
la sua chitarra nel backstage del Pacific
Coliseum, Vancouver, Canada.
*Storm Thorgerson and Aubrey "Po" Powell,
Hipgnosis, Pink Floyd Music Ltd*

37   NOVEMBRE 1974, *Roger Waters*
e il manager della band *Steve O'Rourke*
nel backstage della Wembley Empire Pool,
Londra, Regno Unito.
*Storm Thorgerson and Aubrey "Po" Powell,
Hipgnosis, Pink Floyd Music Ltd*

SOUNDCHECK

39   APRILE 1975, uno dei roadie regge
un blocco di ghiaccio secco, usato per creare
un vorticante effetto nebbia sul palco,
nel backstage della Los Angeles Memorial
Sports Arena, Stati Uniti.
*Storm Thorgerson and Aubrey "Po" Powell,
Hipgnosis, Pink Floyd Music Ltd*

40   APRILE 1975, un roadie si riposa
nel backstage dello University Activity
Centre, Arizona, Stati Uniti.
*Storm Thorgerson and Aubrey "Po" Powell,
Hipgnosis, Pink Floyd Music Ltd*

41   APRILE 1975, *Pete Revell, Graeme
Fleming* e altri roadie trasportano
il grande aeromodello, che volteggiava
sul pubblico prima di schiantarsi sul palco
in un'esplosione spettacolare, nel backstage

del Tucson Community Center, Arizona, Stati Uniti.
Storm Thorgerson and Aubrey "Po" Powell, Hipgnosis, Pink Floyd Music Ltd

42   DICEMBRE 1974, i roadie preparano lo schermo per le proiezioni sul palco all'Hippodrome, Bristol, Regno Unito.
Storm Thorgerson and Aubrey "Po" Powell, Hipgnosis, Pink Floyd Music Ltd

43   APRILE 1975, la security alla Los Angeles Memorial Sports Arena, Stati Uniti.
Storm Thorgerson and Aubrey "Po" Powell, Hipgnosis, Pink Floyd Music Ltd

44   NOVEMBRE 1974, *Nick Mason*, *David Gilmour* e il roadie *Bernie Caulder* sul palco durante il soundcheck alla Usher Hall, Edimburgo, Regno Unito.
Jill Furmanovsky Archive

45   NOVEMBRE 1974, *David Gilmour* e il designer dello studio Hipgnosis *Storm Thorgerson* sul palco durante il soundcheck alla Usher Hall, Edimburgo, Regno Unito.
Jill Furmanovsky Archive

46   NOVEMBRE 1974, *Roger Waters*, *Nick Mason* e il lighting designer *Arthur Max* al mixer durante il soundcheck alla Wembley Empire Pool, Londra, Regno Unito.
Jill Furmanovsky Archive

47   NOVEMBRE 1974, *Richard Wright* e il lighting designer *Arthur Max* al mixer durante il soundcheck alla Wembley Empire Pool, Londra, Regno Unito.
Jill Furmanovsky Archive

48   NOVEMBRE 1974, *David Gilmour* e il responsabile delle chitarre *Phil Taylor* sul palco durante il soundcheck alla Wembley Empire Pool, Londra, Regno Unito.
Jill Furmanovsky Archive

49   NOVEMBER 1974, *Roger Waters*, *Nick Mason* e *Richard Wright* sul palco durante il soundcheck all'Empire Theatre, Liverpool, Regno Unito.
Storm Thorgerson and Aubrey "Po" Powell, Hipgnosis, Pink Floyd Music Ltd

50   DICEMBRE 1974, *David Gilmour* e *Roger Waters* sul palco durante il soundcheck all'Hippodrome, Birmingham, Regno Unito.
Jill Furmanovsky Archive

51   DICEMBRE 1974, *Nick Mason*, *David Gilmour* e *Roger Waters* sul palco durante il soundcheck all'Hippodrome, Birmingham, Regno Unito.
Jill Furmanovsky Archive

52   APRILE 1975, *Roger Waters*, il manager di produzione *Robbie Williams*, il fonico di mix *Brian Humphries* e il sound designer *Bill Kelsey* al mixer durante il soundcheck al Pacific Coliseum, Vancouver, Canada.
Storm Thorgerson and Aubrey "Po" Powell, Hipgnosis, Pink Floyd Music Ltd

53   NOVEMBRE 1974, la corista *Venetta Fields* legge il programma in stile fumetto dei

"Floyd" durante il soundcheck alla Usher Hall, Edimburgo, Regno Unito.
Jill Furmanovsky Archive

54   APRILE 1975, il palco durante il soundcheck alla Los Angeles Memorial Sports Arena, Stati Uniti.
Storm Thorgerson and Aubrey "Po" Powell, Hipgnosis, Pink Floyd Music Ltd

55   NOVEMBRE 1974, il palco durante il soundcheck alla Usher Hall, Edimburgo, Regno Unito.
Jill Furmanovsky Archive

56   DICEMBRE 1974, lo staff del tour, prima fila: *Paul Devine*, *Pete Revell*, *Bernie Caulder*, *Paul Murray*, il tape operator *Mick Kluczynski*, una persona non identificata, il responsabile delle chitarre *Phil Taylor* e un'altra persona non identificata; seconda fila: *Graeme Fleming*, *Coon Thompson*, il manager di produzione *Robbie Williams*, una persona non identificata, *Nick Rochford*, *Mick Marshall* e altre persone non identificate al Palace Theatre, Manchester, Regno Unito.
Pink Floyd Archive

57   APRILE 1975, l'arrivo dei fan dei Pink Floyd al Pacific Coliseum, Vancouver, Canada.
Storm Thorgerson and Aubrey "Po" Powell, Hipgnosis, Pink Floyd Music Ltd

SHOWS

59   APRILE 1975, i fan dei Pink Floyd alla Los Angeles Memorial Sports Arena, Stati Uniti.
Storm Thorgerson and Aubrey "Po" Powell, Hipgnosis, Pink Floyd Music Ltd

60   GIUGNO 1972, *Roger Waters* suona dal vivo al Dome, Brighton, Regno Unito.
Jill Furmanovsky Archive

61   GIUGNO 1972, *David Gilmour*, *Nick Mason* e *Roger Waters* suonano dal vivo al Dome, Brighton, Regno Unito.
Jill Furmanovsky Archive

62   APRILE 1975, la band suona dal vivo, tra fumo e giochi di luce, al Pacific Coliseum, Vancouver, Canada.
Storm Thorgerson and Aubrey "Po" Powell, Hipgnosis, Pink Floyd Music Ltd

63   MAGGIO 1973, la band suona dal vivo, tra fumo e giochi di luce, alla Earls Court, Londra, Regno Unito.
Jill Furmanovsky Archive

64   OTTOBRE 1972, la band suona dal vivo, tra fumo e giochi di luce, alla Wembley Empire Pool, Londra, Regno Unito.
Jill Furmanovsky Archive

65   NOVEMBRE 1974, i fan dei Pink Floyd alla Wembley Empire Pool, Londra, Regno Unito.
Jill Furmanovsky Archive

66   MAGGIO 1973, la band suona dal vivo alla Earls Court, Londra, Regno Unito.
Jill Furmanovsky Archive

67   NOVEMBRE 1974, *David Gilmour* suona una steel guitar elettrica della Jedson all'Empire Theatre, Liverpool, Regno Unito.
Jill Furmanovsky Archive

68   NOVEMBRE 1973, *Roger Waters* suona dal vivo al Rainbow Theatre, Londra, Regno Unito.
Jill Furmanovsky Archive

69   NOVEMBRE 1973, le coriste *Vicki Brown*, *Liza Strike* e *Clare Torry* cantano dal vivo al Rainbow Theatre, Londra, Regno Unito.
Jill Furmanovsky Archive

70   NOVEMBRE 1974, *Richard Wright* suona dal vivo alla Wembley Empire Pool, Londra, Regno Unito.
Jill Furmanovsky Archive

71   NOVEMBRE 1973, *Nick Mason* suona dal vivo al Rainbow Theatre, Londra, Regno Unito.
Jill Furmanovsky Archive

72   APRILE 1975, la band suona dal vivo al Pacific Coliseum, Vancouver, Canada.
Storm Thorgerson and Aubrey "Po" Powell, Hipgnosis, Pink Floyd Music Ltd

73   MAGGIO 1973, *Roger Waters* suona dal vivo vicino al gong fiammante alla Earls Court, Londra, Regno Unito.
Jill Furmanovsky Archive

74   NOVEMBRE 1974, i fan dei Pink Floyd alla Wembley Empire Pool, Londra, Regno Unito.
Storm Thorgerson and Aubrey "Po" Powell, Hipgnosis, Pink Floyd Music Ltd

75   MAGGIO 1973, *David Gilmour* suona dal vivo alla Earls Court, Londra, Regno Unito.
Jill Furmanovsky Archive

76   NOVEMBRE 1974, la band suona dal vivo tra le immagini proiettate sugli schermi all'Empire Theatre, Liverpool, Regno Unito.
Storm Thorgerson and Aubrey "Po" Powell, Hipgnosis, Pink Floyd Music Ltd

77   NOVEMBRE 1974, *David Gilmour*, *Nick Mason* e *Roger Waters* suonano dal vivo tra le immagini proiettate sugli schermi alla Wembley Empire Pool, Londra, Regno Unito.
Jill Furmanovsky Archive

78   DICEMBRE 1974, *Nick Mason* e *Roger Waters* suonano dal vivo tra le immagini proiettate sugli schermi al Palace Theatre, Manchester, Regno Unito.
Jill Furmanovsky Archive

79   DICEMBRE 1974, una sequenza animata proiettata sullo schermo, disegnata da *Ian Emes*, per accompagnare la canzone "Time" al Palace Theatre, Manchester, Regno Unito.
Jill Furmanovsky Archive

80   APRILE 1975, la band suona dal vivo davanti alle proiezioni sullo schermo al

Pacific Coliseum, Vancouver, Canada.
Storm Thorgerson and Aubrey "Po" Powell,
Hipgnosis, Pink Floyd Music Ltd

81 APRILE 1975, *Nick Mason* suona dal vivo
al Pacific Coliseum, Vancouver, Canada.
Storm Thorgerson and Aubrey "Po" Powell,
Hipgnosis, Pink Floyd Music Ltd

82 APRILE 1975, le coriste *Venetta Fields*
e *Carlena Williams* cantano dal vivo alla Los
Angeles Memorial Sports Arena, Stati Uniti.
Storm Thorgerson and Aubrey "Po" Powell,
Hipgnosis, Pink Floyd Music Ltd

83 NOVEMBRE 1974, *Roger Waters* suona
dal vivo alla Usher Hall, Edimburgo,
Regno Unito.
Jill Furmanovsky Archive

84 NOVEMBRE 1974, *David Gilmour* suona
dal vivo alla Wembley Empire Pool, Londra,
Regno Unito.
Jill Furmanovsky Archive

85 APRILE 1975, *Richard Wright* suona dal
vivo al Pacific Coliseum, Vancouver, Canada.
Storm Thorgerson and Aubrey "Po" Powell,
Hipgnosis, Pink Floyd Music Ltd

86 DICEMBRE 1974, le coriste *Venetta*
Fields e *Carlena Williams* cantano dal vivo
al Palace Theatre, Manchester, Regno Unito.
Jill Furmanovsky Archive

87 NOVEMBRE 1974, *Nick Mason* suona
dal vivo alla Empire Pool, Wembley, Regno
Unito.
Jill Furmanovsky Archive

88 NOVEMBRE 1974, *Roger Waters* suona
dal vivo alla Wembley Empire Pool, Londra,
Regno Unito.
Jill Furmanovsky Archive

89 APRILE 1975, la corista *Carlena*
Williams canta dal vivo alla Los Angeles
Memorial Sports Arena, Stati Uniti.
Storm Thorgerson and Aubrey 'Po' Powell,
Hipgnosis, Pink Floyd Music Ltd

90 DICEMBRE 1974, i fan dei Pink Floyd al
Palace Theatre, Manchester, Regno Unito.
Jill Furmanovsky Archive

91 NOVEMBRE 1974, la band suona
dal vivo mentre un grande aeromodello si
schianta sul palco della Wembley Empire
Pool, Londra, Regno Unito.
Jill Furmanovsky Archive

92 APRILE 1975, *Nick Mason* suona
la sua batteria Ludwig, con l'onda di
Hokusai dipinta a mano da *Kate Hepburn*,
alla Los Angeles Memorial Sports Arena,
Stati Uniti.
Storm Thorgerson and Aubrey "Po" Powell,
Hipgnosis, Pink Floyd Music Ltd

93 APRILE 1975, *David Gilmour* suona
la sua lap steel guitar alla Los Angeles
Memorial Sports Arena, Stati Uniti.
Storm Thorgerson and Aubrey "Po" Powell,
Hipgnosis, Pink Floyd Music Ltd

94 APRILE 1975, *David Gilmour* e *Richard*
Wright suonano dal vivo al Pacific Coliseum,
Vancouver, Canada.
Storm Thorgerson and Aubrey "Po" Powell,
Hipgnosis, Pink Floyd Music Ltd

95 APRILE 1975, *Roger Waters* e *Richard*
Wright suonano dal vivo alla Los Angeles
Memorial Sports Arena, Stati Uniti.
Storm Thorgerson and Aubrey "Po" Powell,
Hipgnosis, Pink Floyd Music Ltd

96 APRILE 1975, *Roger Waters* e *Richard*
Wright suonano dal vivo alla Los Angeles
Memorial Sports Arena, Stati Uniti.
Storm Thorgerson and Aubrey "Po" Powell,
Hipgnosis, Pink Floyd Music Ltd

97 APRILE 1975, *Richard Wright* e *Roger*
Waters suonano dal vivo al Pacific Coliseum,
Vancouver, Canada.
Storm Thorgerson and Aubrey "Po" Powell,
Hipgnosis, Pink Floyd Music Ltd

98 NOVEMBRE 1974, la band suona dal
vivo, tra gli effetti laser, alla Wembley Empire
Pool, Londra, Regno Unito.
Jill Furmanovsky Archive

99 NOVEMBRE 1974, i fan dei Pink Floyd
alla Usher Hall, Edimburgo, Regno Unito.
Jill Furmanovsky Archive

100 NOVEMBRE 1974, *Nick Mason* suona
dal vivo alla Usher Hall, Edimburgo,
Regno Unito.
Jill Furmanovsky Archive

101 APRILE 1975, *Roger Waters* suona dal
vivo al Pacific Coliseum, Vancouver, Canada.
Storm Thorgerson and Aubrey "Po" Powell,
Hipgnosis, Pink Floyd Music Ltd

102 GIUGNO 1972, *David Gilmour* suona
dal vivo al Dome, Brighton, Regno Unito.
Jill Furmanovsky Archive

103 APRILE 1975, *Richard Wright* suona
dal vivo al Tucson Community Center,
Arizona, Stati Uniti.
Storm Thorgerson and Aubrey "Po" Powell,
Hipgnosis, Pink Floyd Music Ltd

104 DICEMBRE 1974, *David Gilmour*,
Nick Mason e *Roger Waters* suonano dal vivo
al Palace Theatre, Manchester, Regno Unito.
Jill Furmanovsky Archive

105 DICEMBRE 1974, *Roger Waters* e il
sassofonista *Dick Parry* suonano dal vivo al
Palace Theatre, Manchester, Regno Unito.
Jill Furmanovsky Archive

106 DICEMBRE 1974, *David Gilmour* suona
dal vivo all'Hippodrome, Birmingham,
Regno Unito.
Jill Furmanovsky Archive

107 NOVEMBRE 1974, *Roger Waters* suona
dal vivo alla Usher Hall, Edimburgo,
Regno Unito.
Jill Furmanovsky Archive

108 DICEMBRE 1974, *Roger Waters* e *David*

Gilmour suonano dal vivo all'Hippodrome,
Birmingham, Regno Unito.
Jill Furmanovsky Archive

109 NOVEMBRE 1974, *Richard Wright*,
Roger Waters, *Nick Mason* e *David Gilmour*
suonano dal vivo alla Wembley Empire Pool,
Londra, Regno Unito.
Storm Thorgerson and Aubrey "Po" Powell,
Hipgnosis, Pink Floyd Music Ltd

110 NOVEMBRE 1974, *Nick Mason* suona
dal vivo alla Wembley Empire Pool, Londra,
Regno Unito.
Jill Furmanovsky Archive

111 APRILE 1975, *Richard Wright* suona
dal vivo alla Los Angeles Memorial Sports
Arena, Stati Uniti.
Storm Thorgerson and Aubrey "Po" Powell,
Hipgnosis, Pink Floyd Music Ltd

112 NOVEMBRE 1974, *David Gilmour*
e le coriste *Venetta Fields* e *Carlena Williams*
si esibiscono dal vivo tra giochi di luce
alla Wembley Empire Pool, Londra,
Regno Unito.
Jill Furmanovsky Archive

113 NOVEMBRE 1974, la band suona
dal vivo all'Empire Theatre, Liverpool,
Regno Unito.
Jill Furmanovsky Archive

114 NOVEMBRE 1974, i fan dei Pink Floyd
alla Wembley Empire Pool, Londra,
Regno Unito.
Jill Furmanovsky Archive

115 NOVEMBRE 1974, lo schermo per
le proiezioni sul palco della Wembley
Empire Pool, Londra, Regno Unito.
Jill Furmanovsky Archive

116 NOVEMBRE 1974, *Roger Waters*
sul palco della Wembley Empire Pool,
Londra, Regno Unito.
Storm Thorgerson and Aubrey "Po" Powell,
Hipgnosis, Pink Floyd Music Ltd

117 NOVEMBRE 1974, i fan dei Pink Floyd
lasciano la loro firma su una piramide
alla Wembley Empire Pool, Londra,
Regno Unito.
Storm Thorgerson and Aubrey "Po" Powell,
Hipgnosis, Pink Floyd Music Ltd

118 APRILE 1975, dopo lo show alla Los
Angeles Memorial Sports Arena, Stati Uniti.
Storm Thorgerson and Aubrey "Po" Powell,
Hipgnosis, Pink Floyd Music Ltd

AFTER SHOW

120 DICEMBRE 1974, *Nick Mason*, *Roger*
Waters, la corista *Carlena Williams*, il
responsabile delle chitarre *Phil Taylor* e
altri membri dello staff in un bar dopo un
concerto al Palace Theatre, Manchester,
Regno Unito.
Jill Furmanovsky Archive

121 DICEMBRE 1974, *David Gilmour* con le
coriste *Carlena Williams* e *Venetta Fields* in un

bar dopo un concerto al Palace Theatre, Manchester, Regno Unito.
Jill Furmanovsky Archive

122   DICEMBRE 1974, *David Gilmour, Roger Waters* e il designer dello studio Hipgnosis *Storm Thorgerson* in un bar dopo un concerto al Palace Theatre, Manchester, Regno Unito.
Jill Furmanovsky Archive

123   DICEMBRE 1974, *Roger Waters* e il designer dello studio Hipgnosis *Storm Thorgerson* in un bar dopo un concerto al Palace Theatre, Manchester, Regno Unito.
Jill Furmanovsky Archive

124   APRILE 1975, *Richard Wright* in una stazione sciistica ai tempi del concerto al Pacific Coliseum, Vancouver, Canada.
Storm Thorgerson and Aubrey "Po" Powell, Hipgnosis, Pink Floyd Music Ltd

125   APRILE 1975, *David Gilmour* in una stazione sciistica ai tempi del concerto al Pacific Coliseum, Vancouver, Canada.
Storm Thorgerson and Aubrey "Po" Powell, Hipgnosis, Pink Floyd Music Ltd

126   DICEMBRE 1974, *Nick Mason* e *Richard Wright* in uno sport club ai tempi dei concerti all'Hippodrome, Birmingham, Regno Unito.
Jill Furmanovsky Archive

127   DICEMBRE 1974, *David Gilmour* e *Richard Wright* leggono «The Sun» e il «Daily Mirror» (*Wilson's Market Mission*) in uno sport club ai tempi dei concerti all'Hippodrome, Birmingham, Regno Unito.
Jill Furmanovsky Archive

128   DICEMBRE 1974, *Roger Waters* e l'amico della band *Nick Sedgwick* giocano a golf ai tempi dei concerti al Palace Theatre, Manchester, Regno Unito.
Jill Furmanovsky Archive

129   DICEMBRE 1974, *Roger Waters, David Gilmour* e il designer dello studio Hipgnosis *Storm Thorgerson* giocano a squash in uno sport club ai tempi dei concerti all'Hippodrome, Birmingham, Regno Unito.
Storm Thorgerson and Aubrey "Po" Powell, Hipgnosis, Pink Floyd Music Ltd

130   DICEMBRE 1974, *Roger Waters* gioca a squash in uno sport club ai tempi dei concerti all'Hippodrome, Birmingham, Regno Unito.
Storm Thorgerson and Aubrey 'Po' Powell, Hipgnosis, Pink Floyd Music Ltd

131   NOVEMBRE 1974, *Richard Wright* gioca a squash in uno sport club ai tempi dei concerti alla Usher Hall, Edimburgo, Regno Unito.
Jill Furmanovsky Archive

132   NOVEMBRE 1974, *David Gilmour* gioca a squash in uno sport club ai tempi dei concerti alla Usher Hall, Edimburgo, Regno Unito.
Jill Furmanovsky Archive

133   NOVEMBRE 1974, *David Gilmour* e *Nick Mason* giocano a squash in uno sport club ai tempi dei concerti alla Usher Hall, Edimburgo, Regno Unito.
Jill Furmanovsky Archive

134   DICEMBRE 1974, *Nick Mason* sul vagone ristorante di un treno intercity per Birmingham, durante il tour invernale in Gran Bretagna.
Jill Furmanovsky Archive

135   DICEMBRE 1974, *Roger Waters*, il fonico di mix *Brian Humphries* e il tour manager *Warwick McCredie* su un treno intercity per Birmingham, durante il tour invernale in Gran Bretagna.
Jill Furmanovsky Archive

136   DICEMBRE 1974, la fotografa del rock *Jill Furmanovsky* su un treno intercity per Birmingham, durante il tour invernale in Gran Bretagna.
Jill Furmanovsky Archive

137   DICEMBRE 1974, *Roger Waters* e *Nick Mason* su un treno intercity per Birmingham, durante il tour invernale in Gran Bretagna.
Jill Furmanovsky Archive

138   NOVEMBRE 1974, *David Gilmour*, la fotografa del rock *Jill Furmanovsky* e l'amico della band *Nick Sedgwick* su un treno intercity per Birmingham, durante il tour invernale in Gran Bretagna.
Storm Thorgerson and Aubrey "Po" Powell, Hipgnosis, Pink Floyd Music Ltd

139   NOVEMBRE 1974, *David Gilmour*, il tour manager *Warwick McCredie*, la corista *Carlena Williams*, il sassofonista *Dick Parry* e il designer dello studio Hipgnosis *Storm Thorgerson* (mentre scatta una foto) fanno il check-in in un hotel ai tempi dei concerti alla Usher Hall, Edimburgo, Regno Unito.
Jill Furmanovsky Archive

140   NOVEMBRE 1974, *David Gilmour*, *Richard Wright* e il designer dello studio Hipgnosis *Storm Thorgerson* giocano a backgammon in una camera d'albergo ai tempi dei concerti alla Usher Hall, Edimburgo, Regno Unito.
Jill Furmanovsky Archive

141   NOVEMBRE 1974, *David Gilmour*, *Richard Wright* e i designer dello studio Hipgnosis *Aubrey "Po" Powell* e *Storm Thorgerson* ai tempi del tour invernale in Gran Bretagna.
Jill Furmanovsky Archive

ARTWORKS

143   ETICHETTE PER IL VINILE 1973
Hipgnosis / George Hardie

144-145   PROVE DI STAMPA DI FRONTE E RETRO DELLA COPERTINA 1973
Hipgnosis / George Hardie

146-147   FRONTE E RETRO DELLA COPERTINA 1973
Hipgnosis / George Hardie

148-149   PROVE DI STAMPA DELL'INTERNO DELLA COPERTINA 1973
Hipgnosis / George Hardie

150-151   INTERNO DELLA COPERTINA 1973
Hipgnosis / George Hardie

152-153   POSTER DELLE PIRAMIDI 1973
Hipgnosis

158   PINK FLOYD 1971, *Richard Wright, Nick Mason, Roger Waters* e *David Gilmour* a Belsize Park, Londra, Regno Unito.
Pink Floyd Music Ltd

159   PINK FLOYD 1971, *Richard Wright, Nick Mason, Roger Waters* e *David Gilmour* si coprono il volto a Belsize Park, Londra, Regno Unito.
Pink Floyd Music Ltd

160   GENNAIO 1972 Pagina del «Melody Maker» con le date dei concerti dei Pink Floyd per i primi due mesi dell'anno.
Pink Floyd Archive

Per l'edizione italiana

Pubblicato per
Rizzoli Lizard
da Mondadori Libri S.p.A.

Proprietà letteraria riservata
© 2023 Mondadori Libri S.p.A., Milano
ISBN 978-88-17-18147-1
Prima edizione: marzo 2023

Titolo originale: *Pink Floyd. The Dark Side Of The Moon – 50th Anniversary*
All rights reserved.
First published in the United Kingdom in 2023 by Thames & Hudson Ltd, 181A High Holborn, London WC1V 7QX and in the United States of America in 2023 by Thames & Hudson Inc., 500 Fifth Avenue, New York, New York 10110

Pink Floyd The Dark Side Of The Moon
© 2023 Pink Floyd Music Ltd
in collaborazione con Thames & Hudson Ltd

Le fotografie sono pubblicate per gentile concessione di Hipgnosis Ltd, © 2023 Pink Floyd Music Ltd e Jill Furmanovsky Archive

I crediti fotografici delle altre immagini del volume sono indicati alle pagine 154-157

Cura: JILL FURMANOVSKY
Art director: AUBREY POWELL
Design: Pentagram 2022
Didascalie delle immagini: Tracey Kraft, archivista dei Pink Floyd

Stampato in Italia da Printer Trento s.r.l.